Animal Families

Written by Tom Donegan
Reading consultants: Christopher Collier and Alan Howe,
Bath Spa University, UK

This edition published by Parragon in 2012

Parragon
Chartist House,
15-17 Trim Street
Bath, BA1 1HA, UK

ISBN 978-1-78186-789-1

Printed in China

Discovery KIDS™

Animal Families

Bath · New York · Singapore · Hong Kong · Cologne · Delhi
Melbourne · Amsterdam · Johannesburg · Shenzhen

Put on your 3D glasses and prepare for a close encounter. The animals look so real, you will want to reach out and touch them!

Parents' Notes

This book is part of a series of nonfiction books designed to appeal to children learning to read.

Each book has been developed with the help of educational experts.

At the end of the book is a quiz to help your child remember the information and the meanings of some of the words and sentences. Difficult words, which appear in bold in the book, can be found in the glossary at the back. There is also an index.

Contents

Animal Families

There are many types of animal families and they are all different.

Some animals give birth to live offspring. Others lay eggs, which **hatch** later on.

Ostrich and eggs

Some make really good parents. Others leave their babies to look after themselves.

Some animals gather in large groups, while others prefer to parent alone.

Kangaroo

Some build nests to shelter their young. Others use their own body as a mobile nursery.

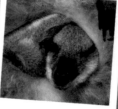
Chimps

DISCOVERY FACT™

Out of all the mammals, including humans, elephant moms are pregnant for the longest time. They carry their young for nearly two years before they give birth.

Elephants

Meerkats

DISCOVERY FACT™

African elephants have the heaviest babies of all land mammals. They weigh between 250 and 300 pounds—more than a big man.

Land Mammals

Land mammals normally give birth to their young, instead of laying eggs, and feed them milk that they produce.

Gray wolves

Gray wolves look fierce, but they are very caring when raising their young. The whole **pack** helps with the chores, such as bringing food back to the den.

Meerkats live in large family groups, called a mob. Older brothers and sisters often babysit while mom and dad are away.

Giraffe calves can be up to 6 feet tall at birth and learn to walk in less than an hour.

Giraffe and calf

Marsupials

Marsupial babies, which are called joeys, crawl into a special **pouch** on their mom's tummy when they're born.

This kangaroo joey is waiting until it is strong enough to face the outside world.

Kangaroo and joey

After spending its first six months living inside mom's pouch, the koala joey is ready to come out. However, it still spends most of its time clinging tightly onto mom!

Tasmanian devils are the largest meat-eating marsupials. They are around the size of a small dog. A mother can keep up to four joeys in her pouch at one time.

Tasmanian devil and joey

DISCOVERY FACT™

Virginia opossums have the largest families of any marsupial, with the female able to carry up to 13 joeys in her pouch!

Koalas

Primates

Gorilla babies learn to crawl at two months and walk upright at nine months.

Chimpanzee moms carry their babies everywhere with them for the first five months. They spend hours cleaning them, feeding them, and playing with them, too.

Baby chimp

Marmosets are very small monkeys that are very caring when it comes to raising babies. The whole family helps out with the chores.

Marmoset

DISCOVERY FACT™

Spider monkeys have strong tails. When the babies are small, they wrap their tails around their mother to help stay on her back.

Gorillas

Rodents

Baby beavers are called kits. For the first month of their lives, kits stay in the family lodge. A lodge is a home made from sticks and mud that is built in a pond.

DISCOVERY FACT™

Porcupines are famous for their long, sharp quills. A baby porcupine is born with soft quills, but they begin to harden after an hour or two.

Baby chipmunks are born without fur, and are blind and deaf. At one week old, they start to grow fur. After a month, their eyes and ears open.

Flying squirrels have skin flaps between their arms and legs that they use to glide between trees. They start learning to fly at about six weeks old.

Chipmunk

Flying squirrel

Beaver

Birds

Most birds build nests out of twigs and leaves, where they can keep their eggs safe and warm until they hatch.

Nest

DISCOVERY FACT™

The ostrich is the world's biggest bird and also lays the biggest eggs. At more than 3 pounds, they weigh 20 times as much as a chicken's egg!

Ducklings bond with their mother from the moment they hatch. They will follow her wherever she goes, forming a line behind her!

Zebra finches teach their chicks how to sing in tune, just like human babies learn to talk by listening to their parents.

Zebra finch

Duck and ducklings

Reptiles

Despite their scary appearance, female alligators are very good parents. The young will stay with mom for a year.

DISCOVERY FACT™

Chameleons are a type of **reptile** that can change color from the moment they hatch.

Pythons are known to be very good parents. They protect their eggs in specially made nests until they hatch.

Different kinds of snakes have very different types of families. Most snakes lay eggs, but rattlesnakes give birth to live young.

Python and eggs

Rattlesnake

Alligators

Male Darwin's frogs help keep their young away from predators by putting them inside the large vocal pouch in their throat!

Amphibians

Amphibians lay eggs that usually hatch into **tadpoles** in water. Tadpoles change into adults through a process known as **metamorphosis**.

Metamorphosis

Frog parents usually leave their tadpoles. However, the male strawberry poison dart frog carries his tadpoles on his back until he finds a safe pool of water to use as a nursery.

Strawberry poison dart frog

Some kinds of toad take good care of their babies. After the female midwife toad has laid her eggs, the male carries them wrapped around his back legs to protect them until they are ready to hatch.

Sea Mammals

Dolphin families are called pods. Family life is very important to dolphins. They work together to hunt fish and care for the young.

Ringed seals live in the Arctic, where the sea freezes for much of the year. They dig caves in the ice to shelter their pups from the cold.

Ringed seal

Every year, humpback whales migrate for thousands of miles. If a humpback calf gets tired during the journey, its mother will nudge it along with her nose and keep it near the surface so it can breathe.

Humpback whales

Dolphins

DISCOVERY FACT™

Sea otters can sleep while floating on the water's surface. Family members hold hands so they do not drift away while taking a nap.

23

h

Almost all fish lay eggs, which then hatch into tiny **fry**. Many fry start life with a yolk sac still attached to them, which they eat.

Fish

Mouthbreeders use their large mouths to keep their eggs warm. They will often carry the fry in their mouths, too.

Many kinds of fish swim together in large groups called shoals. Shoals provide protection from predators.

Lemon sharks give birth to live young, instead of laying eggs. The pups are born completely formed.

Fish eggs

Lemon shark

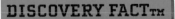

DISCOVERY FACT™

Male sea horses store the female's eggs in a special pouch until they are ready to hatch!

25

Quiz

Now try this quiz! All the answers can be found in this book.

1. How tall can giraffe calves be at birth?

a) 4 feet
b) 5 feet
c) 6 feet

2. How long do chimpanzee moms carry their babies around for after birth?

a) Five months
b) Six months
c) Seven months

3. What are baby beavers called?

a) Calves
b) Kits
c) Joeys

4. An ostrich egg is how many times heavier than a chicken's egg?

a) 20
b) 25
c) 30

5. Which sea mammals hold hands while they sleep on the surface of the water?

a) Humpback whales
b) Sea otters
c) Ringed seals

6. What is a large group of fish swimming together called?

a) Fry
b) Pouch
c) Shoal

Glossary

Amphibians   Animals with cold blood that start life in water as tadpoles when they're born, before changing into adults and coming onto dry land.

Fry   Young fish that have just hatched from their eggs.

Hatch   When a baby emerges from its egg.

Marsupials   Mammals that carry their babies in a special pouch after they have been born.

Metamorphosis   What happens when tadpoles of amphibians change into adults, by growing arms and legs and usually losing their tails.

Pack   A group of wild animals that live and hunt together.

Pouch	A pocket on a marsupial mother's tummy where the young are carried after birth.
Primates	Mammals, including monkeys, apes, and humans, that have hands, handlike feet and forward-facing eyes.
Reptiles	Cold-blooded animals with dry, scaly skin that keep warm by basking in the sun.
Rodents	Mammals with strong front teeth that never stop growing, so that they have to constantly wear them down to keep them the correct length.
Tadpoles	The young of amphibians. They hatch in water and have tails and gills.

Index

Acknowledgments

Images from iStockphoto